Also by Angela Y. Nixon

A Christmas Carol: Charles Dickens Christmas Story Retold for 21ST Century

Trump For Blacks: Highlights on Trumps achievements in the black community

Melanin Driven

What's Up Ngr?

Angela Y. Nixon

JENIS GROUP
PUBLISHING

WHAT'S UP NGR? by Angela Y. Nixon © 2018

Any unauthorized reproduction, use, copying, distribution or sale of these materials – including words and illustrations – without written consent of the author is strictly prohibited. Federal law provides severe penalties for unauthorized reproduction, use, copying or distribution of copyrighted material.

This book is a work of fiction. Names, characters, businesses, organizations, places, events and incidents either are the product of the author's imagination or are used fictitiously. Any resemblance to actual persons, living or dead, events, or locales is entirely coincidental.

First Edition: December 2018

ISBN: 978-1-942674-27-6

10 9 8 7 6 5 4 3 2 1

BOOK COVER DESIGN BY ANGELA Y. NIXON

For bulk order prices or any other queries, please contact aynixon@jenisgroup.com

I wrote this book with my three sons in mind. I dedicate the book to all young and beautiful black men. I see you trying. I see you coping. I see you young black man, I honor you. I promise to encourage you, I promise not to put you down, I promise not to pressure you to fit in or get in where you fit in. Do know it's not easy, for I have been programmed to think about you a certain kind of way. I see you and I feel you. All I want to do is love you. Let's work together, let's build an empire, let us do what you want to do. Do you know what that is? It doesn't matter keeping doing til you find that niche.

God got you and so do I.

CONTENTS

THE "N" WORD 1

THE PARK..23

THE STRUGGLE 47

REVELATION 59

THE CHANGE 73

EPILOGUE 81

THE "N" WORD

"Boy, don't you hear me? I said on your knees! On your knees and keep them eyes open, I want you to see this. I want all of you to see this..."

His voice carried a wicked tone with a sadistic grin to match. I got a good look at his face. He got a kick out of this, I could tell. There was evil intent in this man's eyes. My gut rumbled with terror. A chill swam in the pit of my stomach, a hollow coldness that eventually spread to every nerve in my body.

So this was that numb feeling they talk about. That moment right before everything goes bad and you can't stop it.

"Boy, I said you gonna watch..." he demanded again, in that cruel, husky baritone. He could call me "boy" all he wanted, but

he couldn't make me watch.

No.

That he couldn't do.

I could hear the thud before I felt it. Then the second thud came.

"Boy! You hear me?!"

The third thud. Now there was no pause between the sounds as each came quicker than the last. My heart fluttered extremely fast like it had been spiked with a high dosage of caffeine. Then it froze momentarily. Then it fluttered again.

"Boy, you hear me?!" he echoed, towering over me with his large, ogre-built body. I could see veins pressing through his pink neck as he looked down at me with an inhuman stare. His fiendish blue eyes were iced over with an obvious heartlessness. I was nothing more than a meaningless animal to him, and I knew my fate was sealed.

I tried to snap my eyes shut, but as I tried to . . .

I sprang up from my bed, panting and drenched. Before I could catch my breath, everything began falling back into place. Everything was back to normal. I was in my room again. I frantically felt around on my bed just to confirm. Yeah, this was reality.

"Oh God. What the hell kinda nightmare was that?!" I muttered to myself. I wiped away the beads of sweat that were sliding down my face. A part of me felt a bit disoriented, like I didn't belong here. I kneaded circles in my forehead as if that would cure the fog in my brain.

Before I could even shake the feeling of what I'd just seen, a bang at my door made me freeze all over again.

"*Boy . . . I said don't you hear me?! You better not be sleeping! Get up!*" It was Momma. I was relieved (yet shaken just the same) that it was her voice instead of a lunatic White officer.

"I'm up, Momma, I'm up!" I shouted back, wiping the sleep from my eyes with the heel of my palm. "Dang, nearly gave me a heart attack with all that banging on the door!" I clutched my chest and massaged it. My beater was soaked.

"*It's my door, I pay for the door, I bang on it all I want! Now get up!*" She wasn't playing with me this morning, and I didn't even have to see her raging face to know that.

"Every morning, it's something with her," I grumbled. "Can't just let a king wake up when a king wanna wake up?" But she was right. I had to get up and get moving. Today was going to be a busy day. It's not every day that Renee would be waiting for me. I needed to take advantage of this moment because no telling when another one would come along.

"Wonderful," I grunted. "I sweated right through my sheets," I realized, as I felt the damp patch where my back had just been. "Eh, I'll change 'em later." I rubbed my fingers together to get rid of the moisture.

Man, that dream had me shook. It was almost like I had really been there. Hell, the side of my face even felt sore. I stroked my right temple and cheekbone, where most of the pain felt like it was hitting. In my dream—more like nightmare—the police officer had slammed my head into the concrete when he tried to restrain me. I was sure he'd shattered the whole right hemisphere of my skull.

I swiveled my body out of bed and paused to get my bearings together before I embarked on the day ahead. As both of my feet finally hit the floor, I caught a glimpse of myself in the mirror across from me on the dresser.

For a moment, I almost didn't recognize that face. I ran my fingernails along the skin under my chin, trying to see if my trademark pesky stubble was still there. Yep. It was. Rough as sandpaper. Momma always got on my ass about making sure it was smooth because it'd make me look "refined and clean-cut". But I liked my scruff and I was glad to see it was still intact.

Once my eyes finally adjusted to my twin in the mirror, I saw that same beautiful face I'd lived with since forever. That face with the almond-shaped eyes, the sharp, slender nose, and the "kissable lips" that girls tended to swoon over. That handsome caramel-brown mug looked back at me and I felt satisfied.

"Sup, king. Pushups are starting to pay off," I thought as I gave a little one-two flex in the mirror.

I wonder what Renee would say? Probably nothing. Just look at me with that little look she does when she thinks I'm not watching. I chuckled to myself.

She always does that, like she can't say what we both know she's thinking.

Like I'm not thinking it too.

Just thinking about that face of hers, it's enough for a man to want to become a real man. It's enough to make... I glanced down at my boxers. They inflated without warning and I gripped myself to keep it under control. It was too early to be getting hot in the shorts already. But then again, this was a 'real man' problem for most guys anyway, right?

I got up to fetch some clothes to put on. As I pulled out the bottom drawer from my dresser, I realized I had no socks.

"Dang! I forgot to do laundry again." This made it the fifth day in a row now.

All that talk about being a real man and here I was smelling my socks before putting them on. I mean, it's not like anyone was going to check them so a quick sniff might be enough.

Lifting Thursday's pair to my nose with one of my eyes closed, as if that would make it smell any better, I did what a man sometimes had to do.

Not as good as I would have hoped, but definitely a lot better than I expected. As long as I can keep my feet in my shoes, no one is gonna notice.

Though just to be sure, I sprayed a little air freshener in the insoles and set them aside to give them time to breathe a bit before slipping them onto my feet. As I slid the socks on, I caught that faint Frito scent and winced from the odor. It was definitely noticeable, but not dangerous. Not enough to clear a room.

I put on jeans first, a fitted pair of True Religion that my girl, Renee, had bought me a few months ago at that dope shopping outlet in midtown. Then I threw on a checkered blue flannel button-down; it was the first shirt I saw. No particular rhyme or reason to wearing it except for convenience. I picked up one of my Puma sneakers and inhaled the inside to see if the stench was bearable. A hint of corn chip masked with Febreze would have to do. I grabbed my phone off the nightstand beside my bed and stuffed it in my pocket.

Looking as good as I was going to get for the day, I slipped into the bathroom to finish freshening up before heading out. Looking down the hallway, I saw that no one was around.

"Perfect. A little peace and quiet," I said to myself.

It's been a minute since I could say that about this place, so I thought I might as well take advantage of it and hit up Renee before finishing up in the bathroom.

I pulled out my cell and decided to start a little FaceTime with

Renee. At first, it just kept ringing and I didn't think she would answer. But then she finally picked up, and I couldn't lie. My heart skipped a beat for a second.

My screen filled with that queen's smile, the kind of smile that makes a man . . . My True Religion started to bulge and I had to contain myself. But Renee's deep-set dimples were irresistible when she smiled. So were her eyes. They were a bright amber color with a little green, which only showed when she was in direct sunlight. She had long, wavy, dark brown hair that, when she stood, reached all the way past her booty. I always told people that I had the most beautiful girl in the world by my side. And I couldn't wait to see all of her in person today.

"Are you calling me in the restroom, Ngr?! You better not be using that damn thing! If you are, you're nasty! You know that, right?"

Her giggling told me two things: one, she thought she had jokes, and two, that I had every reason to be excited to see her later on today.

Giggles or no giggles, Renee always liked to give me a hard time. I guess that's what happens when you get to know a person. The better they know you, the more jokes they got.

"I'm not—I mean, I'm in the restroom, yeah, but like, I'm not *in* the restroom. Look!"

Before she could go in on me more, I swung the phone around

to show her the rest of the bathroom.

But my plan fell through as she cracked, "*I don't wanna see you using the restroom! Damn, Ngr, you really are nasty.*" She laughed.

I awkwardly laughed back and kneaded my brow, slightly embarrassed. She always did this to me. Always made me sweat.

My failed attempt at proving my innocence still lingered in the air, as she continued to giggle at my expense.

"I'm not—," I said, still trying to save face. "You know what, I'm just calling to make sure we're still on for today. Are we still on?"

"*Yeah, Ngr, we still on for today. I have to be down there anyways.*"

Renee's tone changed with that last part. I could see that she was thinking about something she didn't want to think about.

That's what I liked about her. There was no playing around and lying. Renee let the world know how she felt whether she wanted to or not.

Though that look, the one where her face would go blank and her eyes would close halfway, was very telling. That look meant one thing: she was burying a feeling.

I couldn't stand that look. It was the same look she got every time we walked past 3rd and Willow.

"What, you meeting another devilishly handsome brother at the park or somethin'?" I only half joked.

"Devilishly handsome? You still using the bathroom, right? Look in that mirror and say you see a devilishly handsome brother in that bathroom. If there is one, give him the phone instead."

That was the thing about Renee. She always had jokes. Even when things were bad, she joked.

"Whatever. You and I both know this face belongs on the cover of magazines," I said while throwing my best model stare into my phone's camera. "Why you gotta be at the park anyways?"

She got that look again, her full pink lips folding in on themselves.

"I told you about today. It's the march for Reggie's little brother."

I had forgotten all about the march. I mean, you can't blame me, right? It seemed like every week, folks were out marching for someone's little brother, someone's sister, someone's uncle.

"We have to keep showing up and letting them know that we won't stand for this," Renee continued. *"That they may get away with it, but we won't forget what they've done."*

Renee sighed deeply and began again. "You know, you should really come with me instead of doing whatever it is you do with your boys. We could use your voice."

Without thinking, I blurted, "Why would I go to something like that? It's not like it matters. Sure, folks get all worked up and shout and holler. But what happens? They *still* shooting brothers in the street. What good a march gon' do for Reggie's little brother? What good did a march do for Trayvon, Eric—"

Before I could even finish being insensitive, Renee got that face again and interrupted with a quiet, "*Wallace.*"

My tongue and throat tensed up. Damn, I wish I would have put on clean socks. At least then, my foot would taste a bit better and not like Thursday's funk.

Realizing that my mouth just said too much, I swept my hand all the way down my face, to wipe away the shame. "I didn't mean that Renee. I'm sorry, I forgot. It was different with your brother. We all made—"

But before my half-assed save could even come out, Renee cut me off and spared me the embarrassment of struggling to find the right words.

"*—not a damn difference. Ia know Ngr. I know.*" She sniffed back tears and I could see her amber eyes turn glassy. She was trying to keep her composure, but her reddening cheeks betrayed her cool. She always said that was the con of being light-skinned. "*Look,*" she mustered up the strength to say. "*I'll see you at the park. I gotta get ready.*"

And just like that, Renee left me standing there with my foot still stinking up my mouth and my foolish face reflecting back at me, as if even my phone knew that a brother had messed up.

"Me and my stupid mouth . . ."

It wasn't even that long ago that it happened.

The look on Renee's face while she stood by her Momma in church that day . . . I swore I would never be able to get that look out of my head.

She had tried so hard to keep it together. Her lips trembled and she bounced anxiously as the eulogizing pastor had said his final words. We sat in somber silence, waiting for Wallace's body to be ushered out of Greater Life Chapel by his cousins and uncles. Renee had already told me prior to the service that she wouldn't be able to handle seeing her brother taken away. Because that would be the last time she'd see him. There was no interment. Renee's mother, Mrs. Gilchrist, had wanted him cremated.

Renee was devastated when the pallbearers carried her brother's casket down the aisle. She'd tried . . . so hard . . . to keep her compartment. But the closer it got to Wallace's coffin being escorted out those doors, the more fidgety and tearful she became. Sensing that her daughter was about to lose it, Mrs. Gilchrist grabbed her and smothered her in her bosom, letting Renee bawl into her dress. She clutched the back of Renee's head, pressing it into her chest while Renee practically screamed.

I wanted so badly to run to her pew down front and wrap my arms around her, to comfort her and let her know everything would be okay. But my legs were cemented to the floor. I was stuck because I imagined if that was *my* little brother lying lifeless before the pulpit. I didn't know what it felt like to lose somebody that close, and I'd feel like a hypocrite if I even *tried* to sympathize.

My consciousness revisited the present. A semblance of guilt stirred inside for not being there for her then. And now here I was making tactless remarks about something so traumatic for her.

'I have to make it up to her,' I thought. 'I have to.'

Thinking of ways to smooth over my not-so-smooth moves, I decided maybe a little TV would help shake the taste of sweaty foot from my mouth.

I trotted downstairs. Making a turn from the hallway into the living room, I could already tell I was in for a hassle before even making it all the way in.

"You have to sit on the floor. It's my time for the TV and my time for the couch." Damn. Just when I thought I had the house to myself.

I should have known my little bro was awake by now. This little kid don't ever sleep in. The sun comes up and this little dude can't wait to start being annoying.

"Oh yeah, it's your time," I said, causing him to grin as if he'd won. "Move it!" I ordered, shoving him to the corner of the couch. "There's enough couch for both of us and your little behind don't take up the whole thing,"

Baby D slouched down with attitude, jutting out his bottom lip like a bratty toddler. I looked at him like he was crazy. He was definitely too old to be throwing passive-aggressive tantrums like this. But if I wanted to, I could fold the kid up like a pretzel and think nothing of it. With his frail frame and lanky build, I think anyone could, really. He was like a wiry, miniature version of me. Same color, same general facial features, but his hair was much nappier than mine. And he had a patch of faded freckles stretching across his nose and cheeks.

Poised to protest and retaliate, Baby D stuck his hand deep into the cereal box he was holding in his lap, pulling out a handful of off-brand cereal and holding it above his head, ready to let it fly.

"You do that, and you'll be eating that freakin' cereal off the floor," I threatened. "Don't even. Plus, you want Momma to find out you throwing food around in this house?"

"I wasn't gonna do it," he said, putting his whole grain weapon back inside the box.

"Oh, you nasty. Now we all gotta eat your hand cereal? Now I gotta have my bowl of cereal with nasty little kid germs? Momma, guess what Baby D did!"

I could see a bit of fear in his face as he wasn't sure if I would actually tell Momma that he just contaminated our morning breakfast.

He was always so fun to mess with. At his age, it was easy to mess with him; eight-year-olds can't really clap back and they're still afraid of getting in trouble.

"Where's the remote?" I demanded as I lifted the pillows off the couch, throwing a couple his way for even thinking of throwing cereal at me.

"Nowhere," he lied, trying to be a smart-aleck. "Plus, my cartoon is on and you can't change it!"

Before I could grab him and take the remote, Baby D, almost in anticipation for what was coming next, took off running to Momma's room, cereal box tucked under one arm, remote in the other while screaming, "Momma, he's hitting me!"

"Little snitch," I grumbled, pivoting my body around to see him bee-lining towards Momma's bedroom in the back.

And in no time flat, Momma appeared around the corner, wide and imposing like Madea from the Tyler Perry movies. She wasn't nearly as old, but she sure was just as fearsome. That "Mammy" stereotype was strong down here in the South, especially Georgia. Momma didn't have the massive grandmotherly spectacles that took up half her face or the platinum gray hair. But she did have the stern eyes, the mean lips that stayed in a permanent pout and that matriarchal sway about her that made you get in line before she even opened her mouth to chastise you.

"Boy, why you making your little brother cry?" she asked, a frustrated frown creasing her forehead. "Hmm? You like being the big man making the little boy cry? You can't share in this home?"

Behind her, Baby D stood smiling and shoving greedy handfuls of cereal into his little mouth like he'd scored a victory.

'He's gonna pay for this one,' I thought. Momma stood there menacingly waiting for me to explain myself, but an excuse couldn't alarm my vocal chords fast enough.

Momma then turned to Baby D. "Go finish your breakfast, baby. But if I catch you smiling when I'm scolding your brother again, you both gonna be crying for real this time."

But before Baby D could try to defend himself, Momma went on, "Don't pretend you wasn't smiling behind me. If you gon' do that, nobody gon' believe you no more. You hear me?"

"*Yes ma'am.*"

Watching Baby D's smile fade from his face with the scolding, I let him slide past me and onto the couch.

As fast as Momma had appeared to rebuke us, she vanished to finish getting ready.

Not wanting to watch whatever cartoon Baby D had lied for, I decided to follow her into the hallway and plead my case.

"Momma, he always bothering me every time I try to do anything in this house. Can't a man just find a little peace in his castle?"

As Momma walked into the kitchen to get some breakfast for herself, she shouted back, "Oh, I'm sorry. I didn't realize you got your own castle! Where is it? Really, Ngr, tell me where it is, I wanna see it!"

Immediately, I knew I shouldn't have said anything. And just like I could see the future or something, she went in on me just like I knew she would.

"Oh, I guess that means you working now and out there buying castles with all your money, right?"

She always went there.

"Because from the look of these blank job applications still sitting on *my* kitchen table, it looks like someone is talking about *my* castle. You know, the castle *I* pay for with *my* job?"

Her words were like daggers driving into my skin.

As she dug in on me, I walked down the hallway and into the kitchen. At least this way, the neighbors didn't need to hear her clowning me.

She pulled a box of frozen waffles out of the freezer and plopped it down on the counter beside the toaster. "Why didn't you follow up on these applications?" she asked, turning to look at me dead in my face. Her brow furrowed with confusion and intimidation. The blood flushed from my head down to my stinking feet in one fell swoop. Here it comes. The same speech she always gave.

"Lemme guess," she said, staring up at the ceiling. "You wanna be like your cousin, right?" Her gaze dropped back to me as she flashed me a cheeky smirk.

She always does that; brings up Trent every time she wants to make a point.

Seriously, it's crazy how you have one cousin that does time and your family will accuse you of wanting to follow the same path every chance they get.

I was nothing like my older cousin. Trent was easily influenced and ever since we were kids, he always tried to fit in with the bad boys, the thugs. When Trent was fifteen, a notorious street gang on the west side of town got a hold of him, took advantage of his desperation "to be down", and he eventually became a part of them. He had officially become a Pembroke Pitbull, named for the infamous street where many homicides occurred.

Before he knew it, he got caught up in an armed robbery case. He faced aiding and abetting charges, which earned him five years in prison. All because he wanted to run with the big dogs.

"I'm not gonna end up like Trent," I said matter-of-factly. "Plus, I mean what's the point of filling out these applications? For one, they ain't hiring and they all for slave nigga jobs anyways."

Stopping halfway at opening the box of frozen waffles, Momma spun around and stared at me. Her dark beady eyes glared into my soul as I tried to hide behind the applications I had just picked up, as if these empty forms could shield me from what was coming next.

Here comes the 'marching with Dr. King' speech.

"Boy, I did not march with Dr. King to have my own son call

himself a nigger," she said, her voice trembling with seriousness. "No sir, I did not let those white folks scream and holler and sic their dogs on us so my own flesh and blood could call us niggers. Don't you *ever* call yourself that or use that hateful word in this house."

"But I—" I started before Momma shut me down with a stare that could petrify Satan himself.

"What did I *just* say?" she asked, putting her fists on her hips. "Don't call yourself that word. Period. When I protested back in '63, it wasn't so that my own *son* could use a word of oppression ... separatism! 'Cause that's exactly what that ugly word was used for! I was nine-years-old when I marched with Mr. King. Birmingham was in shambles and me and my friends, Patsy and Norma Jean was right there in the middle of it. I remember it like it was yesterday." Momma paused and looked away with nostalgia in her eyes. "Patsy's big sister had driven us to where they was demonstrating. In a busted '53 Plymouth Cranbrook..."

"... in a busted '53 Plymouth Cranbrook..." I said in unison with her, giggling under my breath. I knew the story. She'd recited it hundreds of times. Always with a slightly different spin, or some extra detail that she failed to mention before. But her 'King' speech usually had the same general gist. I wasn't laughing at the content of the story, but the *way* she delivered it. Momma could be so dramatic at times.

"Boy, ain't nothin' funny about what I went through to try to make a difference for Black folks," she continued. "You can laugh all you want, but just remember, it was the hell we went through in Alabama that contributed to your Black butt having a real shot at life. A march for *freedom*! Freedom from being subjugated to the white man. Freedom from being treated like scum on the bottom of a shoe. There was *young people* there, many of 'em half your age, out there riskin' their lives so that *your* generation could have it better! You know King even called it one of the most important things that ever happened to America? It was powerful, son. For our people, this meant redemption. And I might be old as dirt with these rickety bones, old enough to be your damn grandma, but I can die happy, knowing that I at least *tried* to make an impact for black folks."

The look on Momma's face should have told me that staying quiet was the best response, but I guess I missed the taste of Thursday's sweat again because without even thinking, I blurted back, "Momma, I said *nigga*, not nigger. Ain't nobody saying nigger anymore beside those tiki torch-carrying white boys."

Yep, there's that taste of sweaty sock again. I guess when you're in the wrong, you might as well go all the way in. And even after all that she just said, pettiness possessed me to still make an ignorant comment.

"Plus, Momma," I said, digging my hole just a bit deeper. "If we wanna say nigger, we can. It's *our* word now . . ."

The look on Momma's face changed. For a moment, it looked like Renee's. There was that same look, before she said, "It's not *ours*, it's *theirs*. Always was, always will be." Momma spat that last word out so forcefully, she nearly gave me the shower that I failed to take this morning. "That word is hatred and pain made audible. I just pray you don't ever learn just how painful and hateful that ugly word really can be . . ."

"But Momma, I'm not usin' it as a—" And before I could even get half my sentence out, she stepped to me, her nose pressed into mine.

"When I tell you not to use that damn word in my house, I expect you to heed what I say," she said, her voice trembling again, but there was a firmness in her tone that made me shut up. She pulled back a little, but was still deep in my grill.

"When you use that nasty term, you speak evil into the air," Momma continued. "*Nigga* is negative. Do you know that those words are cousins? Nigga, nigger, Negro, negative, they all rooted in the same damn thing. Darkness . . . blackness . . . absence. Remember that whenever you let that word slip out yo gums. You're not speaking light into the world, you speaking darkness."

Silence filled the air at once. All you could hear was the ferocious breath coming out of Momma's nostrils. She had worked herself up. And it was best not to say anything once she reached that point. She glared at me with the craziest eyes. But eventually, they settled back to normal, she collected herself, and took a moment to breathe before she spoke.

"Boy, you make me so mad sometimes," she said, lightly chuckling to herself and going to pick up one of the blank job applications. "But I swear I can't just let you fall flat on your face." She showed me the form in her hand, an opportunity for employment at the dollar store up the street from us.

"Dollar Barn is hiring, and I called down there just to make sure," she said. "They said yes, so you fill this thing out, turn it in, and be ready for a interview. I know it ain't the most glamorous gig, but it's a stepping stone. And at this point, you can't afford to be choosy."

She disappeared into the laundry room around the corner from the kitchen for a hot second, and returned with a pink shirt in her hand. Holding it out in front of me, she said, "I washed this for you *when* you have your interview next week. It's fresh, it's pressed, and it's ready for you to wear." Momma practically shoved the thing into my hands.

Unwilling, I took it and fumbled it around in my hand, staring at it with mild disgust. Momma snatched it back from my grasp. "No, boy! What the hell you doing?! You gon' wrinkle it! Here, I'll take it and hang it up somewhere safe so you don't jack it up and ruin yo chances of getting employed."

"Momma, I don't wanna wear that, though," I said reluctantly. "I mean, seriously. Pink?"

"It's *salmon*, boy. Learn ya colors," Momma snapped back. "And ain't nothin' wrong with a man wearing a color like this." She held it up against my chest, closing one eye and tilting her head like she was a stylist. "This complements your skin very well, by the way. You'll look nice. Momma picked this out for you for a reason."

I looked down at the pink polo hanging in front of my torso. "Professionals wear this?" I asked smartly.

"Boy, yes!" Momma exclaimed. "Yes they do!"

"Looks like a golfer shirt to me. Gon' have me out here lookin' like Tiger Woods," I cracked.

"*Country clubber* is more politically correct," Momma joked back, yanking the shirt away from my chest. "And you betta wear this for that interview. Spent almost $20 for this shirt."

"Okay, Momma," I said, with no real intention of wearing that ugly ass shirt or showing up at that interview.

"And please," Momma said. "When you go in for the interview, try not to say n—that word, okay? Think about the evil you put out there when you say it."

That same look, the look that Renee had given me earlier, crossed her face again.

THE PARK

MOMMA'S WORDS and the way she looked before I left, were still floating in my mind by the time I got to the park. I hadn't even realized that I had walked there so quickly until I heard . . .

"Hey, yo, Captain Negro CEO! Working hard, crunching numbers and impressing stockholders, you don't see yo boy waving at you?!"

I knew exactly who it was before I even turned around. Only one person on the planet called me that.

"Somebody gotta make the money and it sho ain't your broke ass! Sup, Tone!" We dapped each other up and went in for the bro hug.

Tone was like me. That's why we got along. In fact, Tone was like most brothers these days, just trying to make things happen and coming up short. It's what drew us together. We never sweated each other's failures too hard.

"So what, you all lost in thought thinking of the shareholders meeting or somethin', Captain Negro CEO? Trying to find a new super Negro saying? Or just wondering if wearing yo drawers on the outside of your super suit is a good look?" He silently laughed and licked his lips. "Cause I'll save you the trouble, it ain't."

Tone loved calling me that, Captain Negro CEO. As if having dreams was a bad thing. I always thought he called me that because half of him thought it was pointless, yet the other half hoped it would happen. Some days, I couldn't tell which way he meant it, so I just let it slide.

While walking over to the dominoes table, two girls from up the street walked by. A slim one and a curvy one. The skinnier one looked like she was mixed; she had long, sandy brown hair and greenish eyes. The thicker one was all chocolate and had a nice romp on her. Neither one of them looked like they were willing to give any nigga the time of day. They hadn't even made it out of earshot before Tone started to spit game.

"Aye, where you walking so fast? I'm right over here, queen!" His eyes surveyed the thick one like she was a prime cut of steak, and he bit his bottom lip, wanting to devour her alive.

They rolled their eyes and exchanged irritated looks, and that just said everything right there. They continued right on walking and Tone waved them off like he didn't care that he just got curved.

"Man, they know they wanna sing a new *Tone with your boy Tone*," he said conceitedly, smirking at his own corny pun. "They just have to act like they're not interested."

That was his favorite phrase, 'Making females sing a new Tone' with your boy Tone, whatever that meant. I'd been hanging with Tone since high school and I'm pretty sure no one sang anything around him.

I hate to say that it was because of his looks, but it was more than likely because of his looks. Tone wasn't ugly per se. He just . . . had awkward features about him that most girls probably didn't find that appealing. Big ears, bugged out eyes, caterpillar eyebrows. He had brilliantly white teeth, though, and was a shade of brown that ladies nowadays seemed to be much more attracted to. And he was a few inches taller than me, so he had a height advantage.

"Can you tear your dog eyes away from girls just for a second and set this game up?" I asked him, as he ran his hand over his greasy waves. They weren't as "oceanic" as mine, though. He had me beat in the teeth department, but I edged him out in the hair department.

"You that eager to lose? Fine, nigga. But don't be crying when

I take them wavy Pumas, dawg. Them is nice, and they gon' be collateral today."

He looked desirously at my kicks and I low-key snickered inside. "Well yo feet gon' be stankin' then," I quipped under my breath.

I think Tone halfway heard what I said, but didn't understand the inside joke and dug around in his backpack for the dominoes. While he set up the game, my conversation with Momma earlier started to ring again in my ears. That woman sure had a knack for planting seeds of guilt in your head. She could say some stuff that would really stick with you and make you *wish* you thought twice before opening your mouth.

"Hey bruh, you look at that video I sent you?" I asked him, mentally pushing Momma's 'King' speech to the backburner.

Without even looking up, Tone immediately shot back, "That nerd ish? You talking about that snakes and a plane video you sent me? Nigga, I turned that noise off the moment that dude came on and said snakes are the future. I'm like, what that gotta do with computers, my nig?!"

Just like Tone. He missed the whole point of the video. But I had to give it to him. At least he was honest about not watching it.

"Besides, ain't the plan to get that app we was talking about up and running?" Tone mentioned. "We was supposed to be launching our own little social media platform, remember? *That's* what I thought we talked about, not becoming the Black Crocodile Dundee."

"Bruh, the video wasn't about snakes!" I snapped back. "He was talking about Python—"

Before I could finish, Tone looked up and said, "Nigga, and what is a python?" He paused. "A snake, that's right."

Trying not to laugh in Tone's face too much, I just continued, "Nah, Python is a coding language, bruh. How do you think you get them apps working, a phone fairy? You gotta program them! I sent you the video so you can learn something useful besides making jokes."

Pulling out the last few pieces of dominoes, Tone started setting up the game.

"Why I gotta learn to code when I got you?" he said, staring at the table, puzzled, like he forgot something. He scratched the back of his head.

"Maybe because you need to bring something to this plan," I said bluntly.

Pushing a handful of white tiles my way, Tone just kept going.

"*I'm* the idea guy," he insisted.

"The app is *my* idea," I answered back.

"Well I'm the nigga that *know* the idea guy. There. You ready to lose, or what, Mr. Black Dundee?"

As I lined up my tiles, making sure that Tone couldn't sneak a peek, I thought about Momma again.

"Man, when you gon' take this seriously? You don't take nothing serious," I told him honestly. Somebody needed to keep it real with the kid, and who better to do that than me.

Tone let go of a sarcastic sigh as he slammed down his first tile, making sure to knock over a few of mine in the process.

"I'm serious about taking your money," he said, clapping his hands together with glee and rubbing them excitedly. "Your turn, *mate*." Tone tried to mimic an Australian accent with that last word but ended up sounding like a cross between a brother with a concussion and a confused British person.

As I went about fixing my tiles before Tone could cheat some more, Tone licked his lips and quietly said, "Look here, CEO, your secretary is calling." He motioned over my shoulder, pointing to someone coming up on us.

As I turned to see who Tone was talking about, I heard Renee's voice shout, "Hey Ngr, over here!"

"I'll be back, bruh. Lemme talk to Renee real quick." I got up from the table.

"Whatever, whipped nigga. Ayo, ask her if that homegirl she was with wanna sing a new Tone," he said, licking his lips.

"Bruh, you can't even hum, talking about singing," I jabbed.

I could tell that one probably crossed a line, because Tone didn't throw one back. Instead, he just quickly replied, "Whateva nigga, just ask her fuh me. Don't be acting all..." before muttering to himself: "Whipped nigga talking about singing like he ain't one whip away from singing *Swing Low*..."

I had to laugh to myself and shake my head. Walking over to Renee, I remembered why I was so happy to start the day. Seeing her just standing there smiling at me made me forget for a moment that I was no closer to becoming Captain Negro CEO than Tone was to actually making a girl sing.

She had a way of doing that. Without saying anything, Renee could tell what you were thinking. You could see it in her smile, like she knew what you were going to say before *you* even did. I think those dimples of hers might have given her some sort of telepathic ability. 'Stop gushing over my cute facial indentations,' she'd say, trying to sound all intelligent. But how could I? They made her look sexy, along with the rest of her figure.

My shorty, Renee, was a literal shorty, about 5'6, with thick hips and thighs that curved into the rest of her legs gracefully. You could really see it when she wore a tight pair of jeans. Like she was today. I glanced at her booty and got excited when I saw how they filled out her pants. Although she never tried to flaunt it, she had a nice body and if she only knew how much I appreciated it...

"Wassup Renee," I said, wetting my bottom lip with my tongue, and biting it hungrily like Tone had done earlier when he was trying to hit on those girls. Yep, Tone and I were a lot alike. "Why you make me walk all the way over here? Just because you knew I would?" She looked at the ground and smiled coyly. She leaned against the rail that marked the boundary of the park, and I slouched down next to her.

"Maybe," she replied, playfully pouting her juicy lips at me. "Or maybe I don't want your dog-ass friend looking at me like a piece of meat at the end of a long day. I guess maybe a bit of both."

Her eyes said that she was only half joking as she looked over my shoulder to Tone. He licked his lips and looked back at us, as if on cue.

"He's harmless. He's all talk," I assured her. "Anyways, he knows you're my girl." As those last words came out of my mouth, I slid a little closer to Renee and gave her a nudge just to drive the point home a little more.

"Okay, well first of all, he's only harmless to *you*," she countered. "Every sister in a fifteen-mile radius got a story about your boy shouting nonsense as they're walking by. Second..." She slid further away, putting distance between us. "What do you mean '*your girl*'?" she continued. "I am not your girl. You know why?"

Trying to hide the smidgeon of hurt beneath a joke, I replied while turning away, "Because you playing hard to get? Or maybe you're afraid to catch feelings for a real nigga?"

Renee's smile said she knew I wouldn't get the point. It was almost like she expected it to go right over my head.

"Nah," she said. "Because if I *was* your girl, you would be my man. And ain't no real man out here playing dominoes with his broke friends instead of working to provide something."

And with that same smile, letting me know she knew what was coming before it came, she continued, "Aww, don't get your feelings hurt, I'm just playing around." She laughed, teasingly smacking my shoulder. "I know what you're really like and if you was anything like Tone over there, we wouldn't be talking."

Inwardly, I laughed at the irony of her perception of me. Because truth be told, Tone and I held more than enough similarities. Yeah, he was definitely much more immature than I was. But we were friends for a reason.

Still, mean or not, jokes or no jokes, a piece of me knew she was right.

"What, did you just come over here to beat a nigga like the police?" I joked, completely forgetting why Renee was even in the park in the first place.

Thursday's funk filled my mouth again.

"That's not funny." Renee's face got serious as she raised an eyebrow just to make sure I understood why it wasn't funny. "As easy as it is to make fun of you, I didn't come here to do that."

She smiled and took a step back, already knowing what I was

going to do before I did.

I reached out to grab her anyway, but she avoided my grasp. "You couldn't be away from this face," I said as I tried to slip my arm around her waist. The distance she made between us almost caused my arm to slip off the rail.

"For someone as smart yourself, you really know how to act dumb," she said, folding her arms and looking off to the side.

Again with the jokes.

She looked back at me with large, doe eyes, batting her long lashes to make me feel a way. "I wanted to give you one last chance to change your mind and come march with me," she said. "You know, it would mean the world to me if you would change your mind."

Without looking away, this time with a more serious look slowly drawing across her face, she said, "You know how important this is to everyone, to Reggie's family, to the community..."

She paused for a moment. "... to *me*."

I knew she would do this. She saw something in me that I didn't see or something that I didn't want to see. But going to those marches really didn't make a difference to me.

'That's the thing about these marches. Everyone comes out, gets upset, and then what?' I thought as I pretended mulling over joining her.

I hopped up on the rail to sit. "How about you skip the march and come chill with me and Tone?" I suggested, pointing over my shoulder to what I could only assume was Tone licking his lips at the sound of his name.

"Ngr, it's important to show up and stand beside each other," she said, grabbing both of my hands and staring at them as she talked. "If we don't stand together, we let them win. They'll know they can do whatever they want and get away with it."

"They do get away with it," I snidely interrupted, causing her to snap her eyes back towards mine with more intensity than I was prepared for.

"I mean, they do," I doubled down. "What's Officer Shelby doing? What's Darren Wilson doing? Sure as hell not sitting behind bars with a brother that got caught with a dime bag of loud."

You would think by now, I would have gotten tired of the taste of sweaty foot. But with every word, I just jammed my size eleven and a half further into my mouth.

Just in time to save my foot from becoming a permanent fixture on my face, Renee's friend, Tonya, showed up carrying signs for the protest.

Tonya was a slightly thinner, milk chocolate version of Renee. They were the same height, wore their hair almost the same (that wavy, hair-still-wet-from-the-shower-type look) and almost sounded the same. But Tonya's voice was a tad deeper, she lacked 'cute facial indentations', and hardly wore makeup. While Renee typically slathered her face in lip gloss, powder, and color pencil (even though she didn't need an ounce of that stuff), Tonya displayed herself bare and natural. She was kind of the "hippy" between the two.

"Girl, they starting without us! Stop wasting time!" Tonya shouted as she slung the signs over to one shoulder.

"Last chance, Ngr. You coming?" Renee spoke softer than before, though I guess I couldn't catch a sign if it was fifteen feet wide.

So instead of doing the right thing...

"Nah, I'll catch you after." As soon as the words left my mouth, any hope that was present in Renee's face sadly faded. "I got business to talk with Tone," I explained. "We got some ventures and plans to finalize." As if using those words would detract from the mistake I was so obviously making.

"If only you were as serious about other things as you are about your plans," Renee said. Her mouth curled into a half-smile, one that communicated disappointment. That last part stung more than I expected it to. Knowing exactly what she meant, I jumped off the railing to close the gap between us.

"I *am* serious about other things." I grabbed her hand to let her know exactly what I meant this time before continuing. "I just have to be taken seriously as an entrepreneur first. Otherwise, I'm just a chump with nothing to give."

That last bit of truth even took me by surprise. For once, I think it took Renee by surprise.

Without missing a beat, though, Renee just patted my hand and gave me a look that almost made me put Tone, my plans, and everything else behind me to follow her.

"Last chance, Mr. Entrepreneur."

Her smile told me she knew what I would say already, so without waiting to hear it, she patted my hand one last time and turned to catch up to Tonya.

As she walked away, I couldn't help but feel a horrible knot twist in my stomach. That was probably the reality of letting Renee down finally hitting me, and rather than making it right, I simply headed back to Tone.

Before I could even sit back down, Tone started, "That Tonya is more than a snack! Nigga, she is like breakfast and lunch combined!"

"You mean brunch, bruh?" I laughed at Tone, who was still unable to tear his eyes away from the girls as their figures got smaller and smaller.

"Nigga, look at you. *Brunch*," he mocked. "Let's meet for brunch and talk about the meeting tomorrow," he said, talking in his best white guy voice. "Susan, schedule my meeting with Eric tomorrow. We'll meet for brunch. Tell him Captain Negro CEO knows a place with the best avocado toast."

As I laughed, I had to ask him, "What's avocado toast? You know nothing about brunch."

"I don't know, but you know they be eating avocado toast like crazy in them brunches. White people will straight murder for it. If they go to brunch and ain't no avocado toast, they be in the streets marching right next to them niggas screaming 'No justice, no peace!' You know what I mean?"

Tone was right. Some folks would lose their minds over the silliest things; brothers dying in the street unfortunately was not one of them.

"Bruh, you better learn to love brunch," I told him. "We gon' be eating brunch with them folks once we make our moves and start making money."

But before we could talk more about avocado toast, we heard an all too familiar sound. A sound everyone around our neighborhood knew all too well. Another one crackled through the air. Then another. Then another, until they started to blend together in rapid succession.

Tone and I just looked at each other. Then the screams started.

Without even saying a word, we knew what just happened. Somewhere close, people were dead.

"The march . . . Renee . . ." The words barely left my mouth when the screams got closer.

"Nigga, we gotta run! They killing niggas! Come on!" Tone could hardly hide the shaking fear in his voice.

"Renee and Tonya, though! They were over there! We gotta see if they okay!" That last word almost stumbled on its way out.

I couldn't bear the thought of Renee... lying there... bleeding.

Before either of us could decide what to do next, Renee and Tonya came running around the corner of the park, sprinting towards us. On Tonya's shirt, there was a large red stain, still fresh and glistening in the sun.

Without another word, Tone and I ran towards the girls, both of us hoping that that stain was from someone else.

"Oh, Ngr, they... they just started... and the guy next to us ... he..." Renee struggled to speak against her heaving breaths.

As shaken as Renee was, Tonya was worse. As soon as she got close to us, she immediately hugged Tone, who looked more surprised than I'd ever seen him, and started sobbing.

"Renee, what happened?! Tonya, were you shot?!" I couldn't keep from shouting at them. I didn't mean to, but my adrenaline had escalated.

Renee looked at me, the heaviness of what just happened still in her eyes. She collected herself enough to say, "No, Tonya's fine ... well as fine as..." Her lack of oxygen didn't allow her to finish her statement. "Ngr, they started shooting . . . we were just marching and someone shouted and then they just started shooting."

With every word she collected herself a bit more.

"The guy next to us . . . he got . . . they . . . it's his blood." She gulped and I could see a knot slowly fall down her throat. I knew that what she had just witnessed was literally tough for her to swallow.

Before she could continue, Tone interrupted her,

grabbing my shoulder and spinning me to face him. Tonya cradled Renee in her arms, knowing that her friend was still distraught.

"Nigga, we gotta go! Like, now!" Tone insisted, a look of utter dread plastered on his face. I'd never seen him like this, ever. He typically played the unbothered role, but in this moment, he looked extremely bothered.

As we all were about to find somewhere safer than here, a Black woman, who couldn't have been a day younger than sixty, stumbled into our view. Looking at us (or through us, I couldn't really tell) with a vacant daze, she started towards our direction before falling face first into a patch of grass that sat between our group and the corner she just rounded.

Without a thought, I ran towards her, afraid of what I knew to be true. I think everyone else felt it, too.

Taking off behind me, Tone, Renee, and Tonya, spurned by

the sight of the elderly woman, came to inspect her well-being along with me.

"Ma'am!" I shouted. "Ma'am, are you okay?!" I tried not to let panic set into my voice, so as not to scare her, but I couldn't help it. As long as I'd lived in the hood and had been around some violence, I'd never seen someone bloodied this bad.

With her face buried in the grass, the woman struggled to get back up, but all she managed to move was her butt. Every few seconds, she'd try to lift her pelvis off the ground, only for it to plop back down.

I took the liberty to roll her onto her back, beckoning Tone to help me. Nervous, he got behind her as I gently flipped her over; Tone was reinforcement to make sure she was let down easy and not rough.

The woman writhed in pain, blood bubbling out of her mouth and sliding down either side of her face. With nothing but a durag at my disposal, I fished it out of my back pocket and cleaned the blood off her cheeks. Her eyes, fading in and out of alertness, fought to stay open and looked right into mine.

"Ma'am, are you okay?" I asked again, frantically looking over her body for any sign of a bullet wound. I didn't see anything, and being that I'd never witnessed someone get shot before, I wouldn't know where to start.

The woman gurgled and glugged on her own fluids before

coughing up a geyser of blood and spit. Some of it almost hit my face, but I flinched in time to avoid it. Grimacing at this lady's suffering, I dabbed some more blood from her face.

"Ma'am, can you talk?" I asked, which in my head didn't sound like a stupid question. But once it left my mouth, I thought to myself, 'How could she, idiot?'

But she surprised me when her lips groped for words. I could see them actually moving. Even her arm rose a little, like she wanted to demonstrate something with her hand.

Weakly, strained, she whined, "I . . . I was sh-shot in my lower b-back . . ." It almost sounded like she wanted to cry. Her finger barely bending, I think she was trying to point to where exactly she was shot. And then the gruesome thought dawned on me that she might have been hit in her kidney or somewhere near her spine.

"I . . . I was tr-trying to run away from the p-po—but they got . . . they got me in the b-back," she further said.

I inhaled sharply and stood to my feet, gesturing for Tonya to hold her while I went to get some help. Anxiously, I twirled in place, looking for the nearest person I could find. Preferably, someone who knew how to treat gunshot wounds. Ideally, someone who was actual emergency personnel.

In the distance, I noticed two uniformed men walking towards us. Cops. Just who we needed right now. Without waiting for them to approach the scene, I jogged to meet them halfway.

"Officers! We need serious help!" I said almost breathlessly. "There's a lady over there who—"

When I got close enough, one of the cops grabbed my arm with force and proceeded to move me back towards the wounded lady. He didn't say a word, but his tightly clenched hand around my bicep sent a hostile message. I figured they had gotten a call already and were here to help this woman. But the looks on their faces hinted a different agenda.

As we got closer to the scene, I noticed the dark red patch on the woman's blouse getting wider and darker, and out of nowhere, a voice yelled out, "Hands where I can see them!"

Fragments of my dream from earlier crept into my head. This was all too familiar.

"I said hands where I can see them!" the commanding voice repeated.

I didn't even have to look to know there was a gun pointed in my direction, but I looked anyways to see who was on the other side of it.

And to my surprise . . .

It was a Black man in a cop's uniform. This moment felt so surreal that for a split second, I thought it was a costume the dude was wearing. That maybe this was some elaborate prank that was being secretly filmed and would probably go viral online. But as I watched this gun-toting nigga fret, beads of sweat popping out all over his pimply face, it dawned on me that nothing about this was a practical joke.

The officer's scrawny hands trembled as he held his weapon. He was clearly a newbie, with the appearance of someone who barely hit puberty. An unsure-of-himself, acne-ridden, soaking wet rookie. Honestly, he looked like he still should have been in high school.

'A brother with a badge and a gun. How could he do this to his own?' I thought, as I looked over at the nervous face that was just inches away from death. The poor lady creaked and gurgled in agony, her hands and arms streaked with blood.

"All of you, hands in the air where I can see them!" he ordered. "Don't make me say it again!"

The officer's voice shook with fear, that same fear they always claim right before they give us another reason to march. Trayvon. Eric. Philando. Mike. Their faces zoomed through my head in a rapid montage.

Between the sound of fear in his voice and the lack of confidence in his ability to handle a few of his own people, I could tell that this young man who held all of our lives in his hands was a baby on the force. That was a bad thing. Because brothers in his position felt like they needed to prove themselves.

Instincts took over as all of us froze, raising our hands in the air, still focused on the woman on the ground. The patch on her blouse nearly covered her entire torso now.

"Get on the ground! Get on the ground! Hands where I can see them and on the ground!"

Without taking his eyes or his gun off of us, the officer reached for his radio with his free hand, clicking through the static to report back to what must have been other officers doing the same thing he was doing.

"I've got five protestors, two possibly armed," he said. "I need back up." His grip tightened on his firearm.

Before he could finish, I shouted, "What?! Call for an ambulance! That lady needs help!"

The sound of my voice must have broken whatever autopilot spell we were in because Tone immediately followed my plea with his own.

"Brother, that woman is hurt! You need to do your duty and call for some help before we all watch a woman die."

At that moment, Tonya, who could not take her eyes off of the woman lying there, added, "We are all witnesses."

Before she could finish though, another officer came running around the corner, gun already drawn and looking for the first person to point it at.

The complete opposite of Officer Can't-keep-from-shaking, the new arrival looked like a cop of inverse proportions.

The sweat dripping down his increasingly reddening face was

not from fear like his young partner, but from having to move more than his large body was used to, though even as he struggled to compose himself he shouted back, "Witnesses to what?! Because all I see is four criminals and the little old lady they just tried to rob! So . . . what did you see?!"

The officer's arrival and answer even caught his partner by surprise, though without taking his gun off of any of us, he turned to address the new face.

"Williams, these individuals were running towards this woman when I arrived on the scene."

Holstering his firearm and walking over to the woman on the ground, her breathing barely noticeable, the officer named Williams placed his boot on top of the woman's chest.

"So these perps were coming to finish the job they started, Fisher?" he asked, applying light pressure with his foot, enough to make the woman's respirations even shallower. I wanted more than anything to rush over and knock the bastard into yesteryear.

Looking slightly confused by Williams' observation of the scene, Fisher darted his eyes from our group to Williams, watching him nudge the woman on the ground with his boot.

"I don't know, Williams—" Fisher replied timidly, before being cut off by Williams.

"It's clear as day, Fisher," Williams shouted. "Those two thugs tried to rob this little old lady for some extra 'scratch' to impress these two hood rats." He gestured to Renee and Tonya with a depraved look in his eye.

"And when Little Miss I've-fallen-and-can't-get-up tried to run away," he continued, "They gave chase to finish the job. It's a damned good thing you stopped them. Pity you were still too late to save this woman."

Without even meaning to, I shouted at the officer,

"Are you crazy? She needs help! What are y—"

Closing the distance between the two of us quicker than his weight would seemingly allow, Williams drew his weapon, pointing it directly into my face. The cold metal sitting on my jaw and the smell of a freshly fired weapon told me enough and made those last words die in my mouth.

'It smells like he's fired it. Recently too,' I thought.

His face noticeably inflamed, he leaned closer into mine, his sharp, pointed nose grazing my cheek. Williams' breath reeked of garlic, pungent enough to make my Thursday socks smell like roses. A sinister crack spread across his face, revealing gnarled, yellowing teeth. He laughed right into my nostrils, his offensive fumes invading my lungs.

My heart sank like lead once it occurred to me that this Williams guy had an awfully close resemblance to the officer in my dream from this morning. Burly build, blond buzz cut, icy blue eyes, and a bearing about him that screamed white supremacy. His beefy neck was raging pink, like someone had just tried to strangle him. The arteries swelling through on the sides didn't help.

"Fisher, looks like we got ourselves the assailant right here," he said, pulling back to size me up. "Coward just confessed and everything."

This time, Fisher didn't look surprised by Williams' lies. He just stayed quiet, his weapon trained on our group.

Sensing Fisher's complacency, Williams went on, "Look, Fisher, I think this one is about to attempt to attack us with this knife he just slipped from his back pocket."

Reaching into his own pocket and pulling out a small Swiss army knife, Williams threw the knife on the ground next to me. With his gun still pressed against my cheek, the smell of its potential filled my nose.

"Well, I don't know about you, Fisher, but I tried to subdue the subject before discharging my weapon," Williams went on, shaking his head regretfully.

'This can't be happening. This kind of thing can't be happening right now,' I thought. My mind was racing.

Images of my little brother throwing cereal at me, my mom saying she was proud of me, and Renee all flashed before me. I was about to close my eyes but before I could, everything went dark . . .

THE STRUGGLE

'THIS IS WHAT HEAVEN looks like? It's darker than I thought it would be...'

Before I could comment on the lack of light in my version of heaven, I heard Tone shout, "I'm blind! Dammit, I'm blind!"

Soon after, the girls began to shout the same thing.

Unless we had all just died and went to the same version of heaven without lights, having everyone present around me meant I was probably still alive.

Trying to collect myself and shout over Tone, I started calling for Renee.

"Ngr, is that you? Where are you?!" Renee could barely keep her voice from shaking.

'This is bad, this is real bad,' I thought as I tried to face the direction I felt her voice was coming from.

As I groped around in the darkness looking for Renee's voice, a sound, almost like a whistle, pierced the atmosphere.

Within an instant, it was as loud as an alarm.

I covered my ears, but it was no use. It felt as if that sound permeated every part of my being, like it was inside and outside of me at the same time.

All the while, it kept growing louder and louder, until it reached an octave that seemed fatal.

The vibrations of the whine caused my entire body to seize. Its swelling volume was relentless.

I screamed in pain, confusion, and just plain terror, but I couldn't hear my voice over the screech of the sound.

The pain and piercing sound combined made my brain feel like it would hemorrhage.

And then . . . nothing. No sound.

Before I could make sense of the silence, everything turned white. Not in color, but it was as if a bright light had taken over my field of vision in a blinding flash. After the immediate flash, everything started to come into focus. However, from the hazy smudges of my surroundings, I could tell something had changed . . .

Rubbing my eyes and trying to figure out what just happened,

I started to stand when something hard came down on the top of my head, sending me flying down onto my knees and blurring my vision all over again.

"Stay down, nigger! Don't you move!"

The voice sounded familiar but changed in some way. It almost sounded like one of the officers.

Still reeling from the blow, I turned to look around at everyone else. As the shapes of my friends gradually came into focus, I noticed we were no longer in the park.

"Where the hell are we?!" Tone's question made me realize I was not the only one seeing this.

Just a minute ago, Officer Sweaty was threatening to kill me in the park. Now it seemed like we were in some kind of field.

Judging from the direction of daylight, it seemed even the time of day had changed.

'How is this possible? Did I pass out?' I thought. The way my head was pounding, I wouldn't be surprised if I had.

"Ngr, what's going on? Where are we?!" The fear in Renee's voice sounded real, so that meant only one thing...

This was really happening.

Turning to the direction from which I heard Renee's voice, I saw that she and Tonya had changed along with our surroundings.

They were no longer wearing the same things I had just seen them in. Instead, they had on dirty, ripped up rags. The amount of filth covering Renee's torn makeshift dress made it look like she had never worn anything else in her life besides that collection of rags.

It seemed like Renee and Tonya were noticing the same things as they looked confused at their new outfits.

Turning to see if Tone was in a similar state, I noticed something. For the first time since everything came into focus, I felt cold. Looking down, I realized why...

I was completely naked, save for a small pair of shorts that were made for a man much larger than myself.

"What the hell is going on? What is this crap I'm wearing?!"

By the sound of his surprise, Tone had noticed the changes, too. He feverishly patted down his garments, mainly his ragged pants that looked like they had been made with sewn-together potato sacks.

Slapping his thighs and then his buttocks, evidently trying to locate his pockets, he squealed, "Where the hell is my phone?!"

His question prompted me, Renee and Tonya to pat ourselves down, too. I had a mini heart attack when I realized I was also phone-less.

"My keys! My wallet! Where is my stuff?!" Renee cried. "What is this hideous thing on my body?!" She examined her clothes with disgust.

My stomach was turning and twisting. I had no idea what was

happening. There were no houses in sight, no playground from the park, no cars driving down the street. The only thing I could make out was what looked like a little cottage in the distance. Something that looked like it was built in the 1800s.

I realized late that my feet had nothing on them. My Pumas were gone. It hadn't occurred to me to look down until I felt something crawling in between my toes. Like a knee-jerk reaction, I jumped out of the spot I was in, and to my horror, there was a pile of ants right where I stood.

"This has to be a joke," Tonya said, nervously looking around her.

"Hell yeah, it must be," Tone cosigned. "I think somebody set this whole thing up and is filming us or something. Prob'ly gon' put this on YouTube." Tone walked out a little further into the open pasture. "Ayo! You can come out now!" he yelled into the air. "We know it's a prank, bro. Just tell us your channel name so we can watch it when this blows up!"

Tonya covered her mouth trying to stifle a laugh, at the same time shaking her head that Tone could be this confident in his theory.

"What if it's *not* a prank, though, y'all?" Renee said. "What if somebody is just really sick in the head, kidnapped us, dressed us in these horrible clothes, and stuck us in the middle of nowhere to see how we'd react?"

"Like the movie *Saw* or some ish?" Tone added. "Some crazy nigga tryin' to play a game with us."

And before we could gather what exactly was happening, the White officer who had pointed a gun in my face earlier stepped into sight; his garments were different as well.

Gone was his police uniform; in its place was a buttoned shirt and loosely fitting overalls.

The pistol he had threatened my life with just moments ago was replaced by a severely worn rifle. It looked like something out of an old western movie.

"Shut up, niggers! Who said any of y'all could talk?! The hell is a *YouTube*? Some kinda voodoo ritual you niggers tryin' to pull on me?"

"Oh, hell naw!" Tonya cried under her breath. "Did he just call us niggers?" I heard her say.

His statement caught me by surprise, too. The fact that he was so open with it was alarming. He was too comfortable with calling us that.

"What're you buffoons doing standing? Get yer asses on the ground! On the ground where you belong! Now!" he ordered, brandishing his weapon to make us move faster.

Unwillingly, we dropped to our knees, totally at this guy's mercy.

"Officer, what is this—" I started before he cut me off.

"Officer?! Boy, what in heaven's name are you talking about? *Officer* . . ." he repeated, shaking his head and chuckling to himself. "*Master* is more like it. Or, I'm sorry, as your kind would say, *Massa*. 'Da massa says we's gots to pick some cotton'," he said, cackling at his insulting impersonation of a slave. An eerie theory entered my mind. What if we were . . . no, it couldn't be. That wouldn't make sense . . .

By the sound of his voice and the complete obliviousness to his new attire, it seemed that Officer Williams was totally unaware that anything significant had just transpired. I didn't understand how. Me and my friends were completely puzzled as to what was going on, so he should have been, too. But then again, maybe *he* was the one who put us here.

"Williams . . . what are you wearing? Wh-what am I wearing? What the—" a quivering voice said from just out of sight.

Slowly, the rookie officer from before had emerged from behind a nearby tree. A quick glance told me he was just as confused by his clothes and everything going on as we were.

"Williams . . . what is happening?" he asked, his brows upturned with worry.

Not addressing the obvious, Williams shouted back at Fisher, "When'd you get as dumb as the rest of them niggers? Just because you stay inside, boy, don't mean I can't put you out with the rest of them mongrels! Now we got work to do! Best do it, Fisher!

Your nigger family here—"

"Whoa, Captain Klansman, you better cool it with that nigga talk. You finna end up on Worldstar talking mess like that."

It was Tone who made the bold statement. I turned to see him stand back up and charge towards Williams.

Stopping him in his tracks, Officer Williams, or whoever he had turned into, quickly aimed his rifle at Tone's head, the barrel coming within inches of his face.

Renee and Tonya gasped pleas to the Lord, while I bucked up to protect my friend. "Aye, bruh!" I said, ready to K.O. this dude on the spot. Without even looking at me, Williams thrust his heavy hand into my chest, nearly knocking the wind out of me. His eyes fixed to Tone, a wicked smile spread across his face.

"Nigger, I wouldn't if I was you. Now back on the ground before I *put you down*!" He swished something around in his mouth and ejected a glob of spit near Tone's foot.

As Williams dug the butt of the rifle into his shoulder and cocked the hammer back, Tone lowered himself back to his knees and quieted down.

"That's a good boy," Williams said, smiling at Tone as if he was some well-trained dog. "Fisher, I thought I said get to work!" His tune switched gears fast. "You best remember who still feeds you! Now take these two big Negroes out to the shack. And when you get back . . . take this pretty one back inside, will ya?"

Williams shifted his gaze from Renee to Tonya. "I'm gonna try this one out while you're gone," he remarked, eyeing Tonya with creepy lust. "So don't rush too much."

Forgetting the threat of the rifle, Tone jumped up and brazenly said, "The hell you—"

Before I could open my mouth to stop him, it was over.

In an instant, Williams pointed his rifle at Tone and just like that, with a flash and a squeeze of the trigger, Tone dropped in front of me.

Just like that, my friend, the guy that taught me how to play dominoes and how to put my weight behind a punch, flopped in front of me.

I could vaguely hear the girls screaming hysterically. My head was swimming and throbbing with disbelief. My sight became watery, yet I could still make out Tone's eyes which had lost their light completely. They were lifeless and empty.

Without even realizing it, I started shaking. Looking over at Tonya and Renee, the expressions on their faces, and the uneasy feeling that settled in my gut, I think we all realized that we weren't in Georgia anymore. This was some warped reality we shouldn't have been in.

"Williams! What did you do?!"

Fisher's voice barely registered. I couldn't take my eyes off of my friend.

"What it look like I done, Fisher? This here nigger had that Mad Negro virus! Well I just saved us all from getting infected with that madness. But by your voice, I think we have another nigger here that done caught the virus."

Turning the rifle's sights onto Fisher, Williams continued, "Now is you mad, too, nigger, or do you remember your place?"

Putting his hands up apprehensively, Fisher slowly backed away from Williams.

"That's what I was hoping," Williams said, staking his long gun into the dirt like it was a flag of conquest. "It'd be a real shame to have to put down my best nigger in the same night I lost my biggest one."

Williams kicked Tone's motionless body over to lay flat on his back. "Well would you look at that, Fisher! Y'all bleed red, too! Almost makes a person think you niggers were actual people. Talking and bleeding like us regular folks."

The numbness of what just happened to Tone started to fade as the rest of the world and its sensations came in like a blaring freight train. Everything was too loud. The sounds of the girls crying, the smell of metal and smoke, and the sight of... I couldn't even come to grips with Tone's corpse lying just feet away from me.

"Fisher, well I reckon your job just got easier. Now you only need to take the one nigger out to the shack."

The shaking within me finally stopped and without hesitation, I shouted, "Do not call me that word!"

Williams' panic betrayed him for a second as he snapped the rifle towards me. This time, I didn't feel the fear of having a gun pointed at me. All I could think about was the speech Momma had given me at home in the kitchen. She reprimanded me for saying how we reclaimed the word. *It's not ours, it's theirs.* Those words replayed in my head. Hatred and pain made audible. I couldn't believe I was actually living the reality of what she was talking about.

My nostrils flared with rage as I drilled my gaze into Williams. In this moment, there was no fear in my blood.

No, that fear died along with my friend.

I looked straight down the barrel and into the fearful eyes of Williams. "Don't you dare call me that!" I carried on. "My name is Ngr, and I am no nigger!"

The alarm in Williams' eyes dissipated as he started to howl with laughter. The initial sound of it caught me by surprise but did nothing to stop my feelings of hatred towards this man.

"Wait, boy . . . so you mean to tell me your name is nigger? Oh boy, a nigger named *nigger*. Well if that ain't just the damnedest thing I've ever heard!" Williams cackled with laughter, but was careful not to take the rifle off of me. I was still a threat to him, whether he acknowledged it or not.

"Well nigger named Nigger, I'm Master named Master and you best quiet down before Fisher has to dig a bigger hole tonight." His thumb skated along the spine of his rifle, sending the message that he could pull the trigger on me at any given minute.

I was no longer afraid of the consequences. Whatever happened, happened. "Not *nigger*. N-G-R. It means God."

Williams howled with laughter again, this time more sinister with each laugh.

"You the nigger god? You don't say!" he mocked, licking his lips and pulling the rifle closer to his shoulder.

"Well, nigger god, where was you when I just blew a hole out the back of this here nigger's head?" he shouted. "Hmm? You gonna raise him up, nigger god?" He sneered at me and shook his head in disbelief.

Williams cocked his foot back and let it fly into Tone's ribs with a hollow thud.

"Hmm, still seems like a dead nigger to me. Guess you ain't a nigger god after all."

Without thinking, I leapt towards the monster that just ended the life of my friend. But before I could extend my hands to meet his throat, the butt of his rifle met my face.

Falling backwards, but still able to see through the pain, I was able to catch a glimpse of the backside of the rifle one more time before it landed harder against my skull.

REVELATION

Opening my eyes, I could feel someone gently caressing my head, the tenderness of each touch telling me everything would be alright.

"Momma..." The words weakly escaped my mouth.

I could feel their hand move away as the rest of my surroundings sharpened into focus.

There was certainly a tenderness in her face, but the woman holding my head in her lap was not my mother.

I felt as though I knew her from somewhere. She seemed familiar; the short, coarse salt-and-pepper hair, the gaunt face and lean body. Those eyes. There was something recognizable about those eyes. They were meek, yet there was something dark about them, like they had tasted death.

An image of a woman dropping to the ground with a dark crimson spot growing on her blouse flashed through my mind.

The woman from the park. My heart sank as I tilted my head to look into the eyes of the woman I had only hours ago seen dying on the ground.

Or at least it seemed like hours. Time didn't seem to make much sense anymore.

Her face looked much more worn than I had realized. While there were no deep wrinkles, I could see a heaviness in her expression and eyes that betrayed her age.

Taking her hands away from my head for a moment to reach for something just out of sight, the woman spoke softly, not taking her eyes off of mine.

"I ain't your Momma son," she told me firmly but kindly. "I ain't no one's Momma anymore."

Sitting up, I realized I was no longer in the field. By the looks of it, I was in that shack Officer—or Master Williams—had spoken about earlier.

Stretching her arms toward me, the woman handed me a small bowl filled with a murky-looking fluid.

"Drink, son."

Taking the bowl from her hands, I decided not to look too deeply into its contents before taking a sip.

I don't know what was worse, the taste of dirt or lead. But either way, it helped calm the burning in my throat that I had been unaware of until now.

Immediately, the scenes from the field began to come back to me as I wiped what I assumed was water from my chin.

"Renee... Tone," I uttered their names thinly, almost with no breath behind it. I had forgotten the horror of just a few moments ago.

Sensing the change in my demeanor, the woman lowered her head, asking, "The folks you came with?"

Already knowing the answer, I nodded to her hesitantly, afraid of hearing a dismal report.

Her eyes filled with pity for a moment before she let out a sigh, shaking her head at the ground. "Son, you best not think about it. Things here are not like other places. Master Williams has a reputation around here. To his face, we call him Master. But among the ones that survive his rage, we call him the Devil."

"Renee..." Her name slipped from my mouth again.

"Was that your wife's name? Was she the one Fisher tried to take into the house?" she asked gently, moving closer to place her hand on my shoulder, as if her touch could somehow cushion what she was about to say next.

"Tried? What do you mean *tried*?" I felt a small ounce of hope spark in my chest as I connected my gaze with hers, hoping to hear something that might be considered good news. But the look in the woman's eyes extinguished that spark.

"Yes. *Tried*," she repeated. "Fisher said she ran into the field after Master gave you the butt end of his rifle."

That sounded like good news to me. Seemed to me like she got away. So then why did she still look like the worst part was coming? I was desperately trying to make sense of what this woman was telling me before she actually told me.

"So she escaped?!" I lit up with anticipation.

The woman let out another sad sigh.

"No one escapes from here, son. No one. If the Master's rifle don't make sure of it, those mongrels he keeps chained up over there will."

Following her finger to where it pointed outside, I saw a shack, not much different than this one. Outside of it were four silhouettes of dogs big enough to be wolves. Even from this distance, I could see they were fighting over something. Afraid to get a better look at what they were tearing apart, I returned my gaze back to the woman.

"Like I said son, it's best not to think about it. If you do, you won't make it here."

Tears began falling from my face as I couldn't help but think about Renee. A knot formed in the pit of my stomach as I wondered which grisly fate she was met with. Either she was ripped apart by those hungry canines across the way or she was gunned down by the Devil incarnate.

"I don't belong here though . . ." I said. The words stumbled out against my intentions.

"No one does, son. No one belongs here. But it's the way it is and it's the way it's gonna be. You best accept that for a fact of life because there are only two types of our folk here. Those that accept the facts and the dead."

As she continued, she reached for my hand and placed it in between both of hers.

"Now you seem to be a strong one," she noted. "I can see the Lord made you different. I know this is hard, but believe me, son, this is a test. If you stay strong and free in here . . ." She let go of my hand, placing a finger against my temple. ". . . then you'll make it. What's more, you'll help others make it. There's glory in helping others overcome their difficulties, and there's more glory in staying strong when others fall. But only if you use that strength to pick up the ones weaker than yourself. You can do that."

Her words hit me, in a way that I didn't expect or want them to. It stirred in me a weird mix of emotions; guilt, empowerment, hope, sadness. I couldn't explain it, but it just made me think about everything. How I'd acted with Momma, how I'd been shirking responsibility, how I'd carelessly adopted a word that carried negativity.

"What's your name, son?" the woman asked me.

"Ngr," I replied.

"Ngr," she repeated, looking off musingly as her lips curled into a smile. She hummed with amusement. "You realize how much power your name holds? Your name is synonymous with god, royalty, king... you are superior, not inferior. Far from it, my boy. I may not be your momma, but if I was... I think I'd have named you Ngr, too."

Her hand lovingly caressed my face; her eyes gleamed with maternal care. "Now it all makes sense. Why I can see the strength in you. There's a special divinity that lies inside of you." She poked my chest where my heart was.

It was odd. This woman didn't talk like how I imagined a typical slave to talk. I mean, she seemed like she had her moments. But she was so wise, so insightful. A bit too much almost.

She got up, disappeared for a moment, then returned with a piece of bread in her hand. Extending it to me, she said, "Here, eat this. It ain't much, but it'll help give you a little energy, something to keep you afloat."

With reluctance, I took it, a bit paranoid about how it would taste. Raising it to my lips, I noticed the subtle smell of whole grain, authentic wheat. I knew it would taste bland, and it did. It was just baked flour inside my mouth. Nothing flavorful about it.

"I knew you'd enjoy it," the woman teased, chuckling. She sat on her wooden chair and dragged it closer to where I was sitting. "I wanna tell you a story. Of a young man who was gorgeous, ambitious, influential . . . a noble African king who ruled over a thriving nation back in the motherland. The country flourished under his rule. It had the most productive crops, it was teeming with rich commodities, it was situated in an ideal area with diverse wildlife . . ."

So far, the story kind of sounded too good to be true, but I kept listening.

"This young king saw to it that his people prospered," she went on. "And he never let *anything* . . . and I mean anything . . . disrupt the peace of his subjects. He was a man of self-control, but he was also a warrior. And he'd rise up when need be. When those colonizers came in, trying to conquer, he would not have it, and he stood his ground. He assembled a whole navy that warded off the oppressors. And not one of his own was captured or killed. Life continued like it always had. Peaceful and undisturbed. Believe it or not, there were tribes back in the homeland who resisted enslavement. Oh no, they weren't havin' it."

A part of me wondered if this story was fictional, if it was just told to me to make me feel better about being Black. About being a descendant of a "majestic" people.

But no matter how much wisdom this woman imparted, or how glamorous her African motherland fairytales seemed, the reality of being stuck here, of losing my friends, of never being able to see my Momma again, of never watching my little brother grow up, of never being able to prove the man I am to Renee, of everything I would never be able to do, began to sink in.

"No . . . this can't be happening." I pinched the bridge of my nose in disbelief at how my entire life had been upended. Squeezing the skin between my brows tightly was scarcely enough to keep anymore tears at bay.

Placing her hand back on my shoulder, the woman tried to comfort me. "It's happening, son. You best calm yourself before you hurt yourself. You took a couple hard ones."

Not heeding her advice, I jumped to my feet, pacing around the dirt floor.

"NO! This isn't happening, this can't be happening! I'm not supposed to be here! What is going on?!"

Each word made my lungs constrict without warning, but I couldn't sit back down.

"Son, are you listening? You need to sit, you need to calm yourself. Please, son."

But despite her pleas and the growing tightness in my chest, I couldn't stop myself.

"I'll never see Renee again. It's my fault she was here. It's my fault that Tone died . . ." The self-blame hit me like a stroke of lightning; unexpected and stinging.

The tightness in my chest continued until it felt like I couldn't draw another breath. Everything started to turn bright white. I tried to balance myself, but my vision was already getting blurry.

Unable to stand or breathe, the ground rushed up to greet me. My head crashed into the dirt, the impact sending awful vibrations through my skull. Everything in my sight grew dimmer.

I could faintly hear the woman talking to me.

"Calm down, son, it's alright. You're gonna be alright. Breathe. Just breathe."

Her voice became distant, like I was falling away from her, as I struggled to continue forcing air into my lungs. The tightness was substituted by a burning sensation, a burning that crept from my chest out towards my fingers and feet.

"Can you hear me, son . . ." Her voice was soothing but muffled, almost like she was talking to me through water.

And then the burning took over my entire body. It felt as if someone had lit a fire inside of me. Every atom of my flesh hurt until the darkness came. Growing from the center of my vision and extending outward slowly, the darkness became larger with each breath I couldn't take.

Then I felt myself descend into the dark . . .

I woke up (or at least I thought I did) on the floor of what looked like a luxurious palace. I couldn't fully tell since my vision was foggy and everything seemed unnaturally bright. Blinking a few times, the shapes around me gradually sharpened into focus. Surrounding me were golden pedestals, hanging tapestries with tribal patterns on them, bronze lion statues, and arranged in a perfect circle were several thrones.

I could tell people were sitting on them, but I couldn't quite make out their appearance. They all looked Black, though. Cautiously and slightly afraid, I stood to my feet and looked around me, trying to figure out where the hell I was. I was honestly tired of adjusting to these strange new worlds. First the slave universe, now one that looked like the kingdom of Wakanda. What alternate reality was next?

Before I could make sense of my location, a set of large double doors swung open behind me. I turned around to find a gorgeous young lady, who looked not much older than me, entering the room. She had a frizzy, dark brown mane of hair which was crowned with a purple headdress trimmed in gold. The headpiece matched the robe she was wearing, except it was a slightly darker shade of purple. Her creamy skin gleamed like fine honey. She didn't walk into the room, but rather, she floated in. As she drew closer towards me, I noticed something about her face. They had cute indentations. Just like Renee's.

She got close enough to where I thought she would kiss me, but instead, she simply smiled, deepening her dimples and revealing a row of perfectly white teeth. Raising her hand to my face, she softly caressed it.

"You are in the presence of true royalty," she said, and the next thing I knew, I was transported to the very center of the circle of thrones. Given that I didn't remember actually walking over to them, I figured this must have been a dream, where physics didn't apply. Made sense, because I didn't feel entirely grounded here.

Encircling me was a jury of king and queens, all with varying shades of melanin. Some were dark chocolate, some milk, a few who were coffee-toned, others who had a golden biscuit complexion. The spectrum was diverse. But no matter what color they were, they all sat proudly and with power. Pigment was irrelevant here.

"Ngr," said the woman who reminded me of Renee. "You are meant to be one with us." She stretched out her arm towards a vacant space beside her, and instantly, a throne that resembled the others materialized from thin air. "Take your seat," she invited. Engraved on the fringe of her headdress, I saw her name: Nkombe.

Bashful, I looked around at the beaming royal faces, their smiles egging me on to take my place among them.

"Don't delay, my boy," boomed a tall, older man with a silver goatee that nearly reached down to his chest. He had a voice like that of God himself. "This is where you belong." A wide grin spread across his face, as he, too, gestured towards the kingly chair apparently designated for me.

I edged towards it, but self-consciousness took over as I looked down at my garments. With these slave rags, was I even worthy— my heart sank.

They were gone. Those hideous patchwork shorts were gone.

Taking their place was a long red robe trimmed in gold at the sleeves, neckline and hem. Then I felt something on my head. A crown, probably of the same color as my robe. I smiled, pleasantly surprised at the magical wardrobe change, and took my rightful seat.

The others stared at me with silent excitement, like there was a secret or something they wanted to tell me so badly. I noticed that on each of their seats were various inscriptions; they looked like different languages. One looked like your typical African dialect, another was Arabic, another was Hebrew, another was French, another had hieroglyphics. I couldn't begin to figure out what any of them meant, but I gathered that each of these nobles sitting before me hailed from different lands.

"So Ngr," Nkombe said, taking a sip of something out of a brass goblet. Where she got it from, I couldn't tell you. "How is your kingdom faring these days?"

Her question caught me off guard. I felt the eyes of my . . . colleagues . . . closing in on me. They wanted to know. I swallowed a knot and my mind raced for an answer. But nothing came to me quick enough. And before I could even start to reply, everything around me seemed to be getting farther away, like I was shrinking. The room and all its contents became blurrier and dimmer, until my vision went completely black . . .

THE CHANGE

" . . . CAN YOU HEAR ME, son?"

The sound of a familiar voice pulled me from the darkness. It felt like I'd been pulled from the depths of the ocean. I could feel the force of some invisible matter rushing past my body, the pressure of my surroundings growing lighter.

The voice spoke more forcefully. "Can you hear me, son?"

And as sudden as emerging from water, everything around me sprang into focus: the sounds, the sights, everything became clear.

The first thing my eyes focused on made me nearly shout in joy.

Tone's eyes, still full of life, were giving me a strange look as he moved his fingers in front of my face.

"Yo, son . . . you hear me? Earth to Captain Negro CEO. Come in, nigga."

Only one person on the planet called me that . . . It was Tone! Alive and talking! I wanted to leap to my feet and wrap my arms around him. But I realized I was lying down. On a gurney. In the back of an ambulance. We weren't moving, though.

A sharp sting surged from the back of my head down my spine, then back up again. My whole brain was throbbing against my skull. I grumbled with agony as I tried to shift my body to a less awkward position.

"Hey, hey . . . easy," Tone said, putting a hand on my shoulder and gently pushing me back down. "One of the EMTs said you still fragile, so no sudden movements."

"W-what happened?" I asked in a feeble voice, my sight still adapting to this new universe. I'd hoped this was the right one, the one with PS4s, Facebook and hip-hop.

Tone gulped before letting me in on the truth. "My man, you took a bad blow to the dome," he said, his eyes carrying this grave look. "That crazy officer who tried to set you up . . . he . . . he, uh . . ." Tone looked down, fumbling with his fingers, clearly still traumatized. "He tried to kill you. He punched you square in the face to knock you out, then he tried to shoot . . ." Tone lost his footing again, turning nauseous as he recollected what happened.

". . .he tried to shoot you in the head. But he was gonna frame you. He asked the other officers to help him arrange the scene to make it look like you were the main suspect in robbing that old lady. But you've been out like a light for the last twenty minutes. I honestly didn't think you'd wake up again. Thankfully, the paramedics checked your head and they said there's no threat of a concussion. But you still sustained quite a bit of damage, so they need to get you to the hospital ASAP."

Twenty minutes, he said. Where I had just gone to and come from, it felt like much longer than twenty minutes. Immediately, I thought about that woman dying on the ground, covered in blood and clinging to life by a thread. Then I got the image of her holding me, caressing me, in that little slave shack. "How is she?" I asked.

A regretful look came over Tone's face. "She didn't make it, Ngr," he said.

My heart froze in place and my throat closed up. Catching a glimpse out the back windows of the ambulance, I realized we were still near the park. This was the last place I remembered before I was teleported to the past.

I saw a couple of paramedics tending to some people on the ground. I assumed others who had somehow gotten involved in the commotion. "Where's Renee and Tonya?" I asked.

"They're safe," Tone said. "Another squad car came, one with *good* cops, and took them down to the station for questioning. They're fine."

I closed my eyes and breathed a sigh of relief. "Thank goodness. And thanks for riding with me, man. I really appreciate it."

"Of course, bruh! We're brothers. I'm right here for you," Tone said.

"I'm so glad you're okay!" I exclaimed, tears bubbling up to my eyes. And without thinking, I rose up off the stretcher and grabbed my best friend like I hadn't seen him in centuries.

"Well I *was* okay until you tried to cop a feel on me," Tone answered in surprise, grabbing my shoulders and shoving me back down on the gurney. "What the hell got into you?" Tone frowned, straightening out his hoodie. "We brothas and all, but there's still a *bro* code, you feel me? Can't be molesting niggas, now." He laughed.

Nigga. The sound of that word brought everything I had just left behind rushing back to me again.

Letting my smile fade from my face, I asked Tone, "Could you not call me that word?"

A confused Tone shot back at me, "*Nigga*? Don't call you *nigga*? What, you ain't black no more?"

Knowing he wouldn't understand what just happened (and how could he—*I* didn't even understand it), I just placed my hand on his shoulder.

"We aren't that word. They used that word when they were beating us, killing us, and treating us worse than animals. But we were never that word. We are so much better than that word."

I was preaching at this point and I could tell it was kind of going over my friend's head. The confusion on Tone's face just worsened.

"Alright nig—I mean, Ngr . . . alright. I don't know what you on about, but sure. Look, you tryna lose some money at dominoes, or what, Ngr? I mean, that is, when you get better and erry'thang." He chuckled. "Not tryin' to rush you or nothin', but I sure do miss whoopin' yo ass when we play with the bones."

He emphasized my name either to mock me or drive the point home, though it didn't matter to me. I had more important things to do than correct him.

Without warning, the ambulance doors swung open and an EMT stepped inside. His abrupt entrance startled me.

"Hey, I'm sorry it took me so long," he said to me and Tone, switching out his bloodied gloves for new ones. "Some of those protestors out there got some really nasty injuries. We gotta get backup and quick."

As I stared at him, I got this weird feeling in the pit of my stomach. He looked just like the tall older man in my . . . dream? The one who had the voice of a god. Except he had no goatee.

The paramedic rummaged in a bin behind me for medical

materials, producing a pad of gauze, some tape and some alcohol.

"Alright, son, this is gonna sting," he warned, dabbing a cloth with alcohol and pressing it against a wound I didn't even know existed until now. It burned like hell, like someone forcing a hot coal into my skin. There was a small gash cutting across my collar bone. It didn't look too bad, but it was bad enough.

"I did not mean to leave this cut unattended for this long, son, I apologize," the paramedic said. "We just had to get your friends out there taken care of."

I weakly lifted my head to see the other protestors through the ambulance windows. Another EMT was caring for them in the meantime until reinforcement arrived.

"Those poor folks," he went on, placing the gauze over my bloody wound and fastening it down with tape. "Just trying to make a difference in this crazy world. And they end up getting attacked for it." He shook his head and patted down my bandage. "I think you're good for now, kid. Just take it easy and don't move around too much. We'll get you to the hospital soon, alright? We should've been had you outta here."

In the distance, I could see one of the participants from the march getting taken up on a stretcher. Finally, another ambulance had come to accommodate the others. As my eyes focused in on the person lying on the gurney, I noticed how frizzy and large her hair was. She was light-skinned, almost resembling Renee. Her face was unclear, but there was an odd familiarity about her.

Nkombe?! Against the paramedic's instructions, I quickly rose up to get a better look. Tone must have realized what I was trying to look at.

"You okay, nig—I mean, Ngr? You know that girl, or something?" he asked, pointing his thumb over his shoulder.

"I . . . I don't know," I replied. "I feel like I might know her."

"From where?" Tone asked. I looked at him, confused and still in this mentally clouded state.

I didn't know what was happening, but I felt like the universe was sending me a message. And starting today, with this moment, I needed to change things . . .

EPILOGUE
NEW DAY

"You've practiced this a million times. You got this!" I said to myself.

Calming my nerves, I stepped out from the darkness and up to the podium before me. As applause roared throughout the auditorium, I steadied myself to give the speech I had rehearsed so many times.

'Time to do this,' I thought.

Stepping up to the mic I began:

"I want to thank everyone for coming out tonight. Truly. Without all of you, none of this would have been possible. A huge thank you to my fellow mentors who put in the work to make sure that our program continues being successful. And of course, a big thank you to all the amazing young men and women who have decided to take control of their lives and make their dreams come true. All of this is for you guys."

"Thank *you*, Mr. Ngr!" The shout from the crowd made me chuckle, but I continued.

"Making the decision to take the hard path, the path that leads to struggling to learn new skills, the path that leads towards long hours spent practicing, and the path that ultimately will lead you to success is never easy. No, the easy path is accepting that which society has branded as being correct. But none of us are here

because we prefer the easy path."

Scanning the room, my eyes caught Renee's, whose smile said everything I needed for her to tell me, even without a single word.

"But we're not the only ones to take this path," I went on. "For generations, our people have had to face a difficult decision each day. Either accept the social structures and systems that were set up for them to fail. Or take charge of their lives and blaze a path for the ones to come. A path that we walk on today."

This is it, you're doing good, Ngr. Keep it going.

"I won't lie. I don't need to, but you all know very well how the cards were stacked against many of us from the start. We've all lived through and continue to live through the obstacles placed before us simply because of our heritage. But like the ones before us, we have something to aspire to, some goal to attain. That we may make the world a little better than we found it. That the next generation after us will not have to struggle as hard as we did to be accepted."

A few claps erupted from the silence, causing me to lose cadence, but still I went on.

"My wife and I started this program to give young men and women the chance they deserve, a chance they are often denied simply because of circumstances outside of their control. In the spirit of providing the youth with another option besides fitting into the mold society left for them, the Young Entrepreneurs was founded."

Feeling pride at the knowledge of how far I had come, I paused before going on. It was incredible to think of the strides I'd made since my crazy incident in the park that day. That experience, which occurred over eight years ago, still held so much gravity in my life. But I never let it stop my grind.

I pursued my dream of becoming a successful coder. Tone (who sings by the tune of Antonio now) partnered with me and we went on to develop several popular social media apps. As of lately, they have surpassed the "Big 3" (Facebook, Instagram, Twitter) in the number of downloads. For the last two years, I've been touring urban high schools all over the country, empowering young Black pupils to also follow their dreams.

"Our philosophy of moving forward through strife and teaching you young ones the skills you'll need to realize your dreams, has been more than just something to do every day when we wake up," I continued. "It has become an opportunity to change the narrative, to change our story as a people. A major key to doing that is to speak positivity into our lives. Words exert so much power. Not to get preachy, but if y'all went to Sunday school, I'm sure you know how the Word says that the tongue is a sword. Well, it is. Your speech, the things you speak into the ether, wields so much influence. What you say and how you say it can drastically change your life. That's why we have to watch what comes out of our mouths. Because we could be speaking garbage and not even realize it." I paused again to let that sink in.

"So I charge all of y'all here right now to help in making a world in which the great men and women who came before us would be proud of. Thank you to everyone who has been a part of making that goal a reality. Now let's have some fun tonight and carry that dream forward in our hearts!"

www.ingramcontent.com/pod-product-compliance
Lightning Source LLC
Chambersburg PA
CBHW060102230426
43661CB00033B/1398/J